FROM BEGINNER TO PRO: HOW TO BECOME A NOTARY PUBLIC

LEARN THE SECRETS OF HOW TO BECOME A NOTARY PUBLIC

By

JACKSON CARTER

Copyright © 2018

What is a Notary?

Ever wondered who are these people authenticating your affidavit, bank documents and legal papers of other sort? Yes, you got that right, Notaries!

Notaries are certified witnesses without necessarily having any law-oriented degree. The requirements of becoming a notary may vary from state to state. Notaries usually make money by charging fees for their service and are not paid by any third party. Certain public notaries may provide services without costing you a penny, out of goodwill. A notary identifies the signer of any legal document to deter scams in legal processes.

A notary can either meet the client in person for notarization or via a video call. Yes, with today's technology where everything can be done while setting at a remote distance, online notarization is also a thing. Notaries after their authentication can provide services using their phone without having to travel to meet the client. There are a multitude of websites available that connect you with reliable notaries around the globe online.

However, different state policies may demand certain requirements to be fulfilled for notarization.

TABLE OF CONTENTS

What is a notary?

Table of Contents

Legal Notes

What is a notary?

Functions of a notary

What documents need to be notarized?

What does it mean to get a document notarized?

Why should you consider becoming a notary?

Misconceptions about notaries

How do I become a notary?

Establishing an Identity For Your Notary Business

Protecting Yourself As a Business

Notary supplies

How to stay organized?

The Checklist to Become A Notary

Frequently Asked Questions

Starting your own notary business

Checklist for getting yourself organized

Building your brand

Develop your marketing strategy

Things to consider after you have developed your own notary business

Final thoughts

About The Author

Other Books By Jackson Carter

Legal Notes

From Beginner to Pro: Becoming a Notary Public

© 2018 Broad Base Publishing

All rights reserved. No portion of this book may be reproduced in any form without permission from the publisher, except as permitted by U.S. copyright law. For permissions contact:

BroadBasePublishing@Gmail.com

WHAT IS A NOTARY?

Ever wondered who are these people authenticating your affidavit, bank documents and legal papers of other sort? Yes, you got that right, Notaries!

Notaries are certified witnesses without necessarily having any law-oriented degree. The requirements of becoming a notary may vary from state to state. Notaries usually make money by charging fees for their service and are not paid by any third party. Certain public notaries may provide services without costing you a penny, out of goodwill. A notary identifies the signer of any legal document to deter scams in legal processes.

A notary can either meet the client in person for notarization or via a video call. Yes, with today's technology where everything can be done while setting at a remote distance, online notarization is also a thing. Notaries after their authentication can provide services using their phone without having to travel to meet the client. There are a multitude of websites available that connect you with reliable notaries around the globe online.

However, different state policies may demand certain requirements to be fulfilled for notarization.

FUNCTIONS OF A NOTARY

There are two functions that a notary can perform that are briefly described below:

Notary acknowledgment

One of the functions that a notary can perform is the verification of the signer's identity. A Notary makes sure that the person signing the document is the person whose name is mentioned in the document. This is termed as notary acknowledgement. Notary acknowledgment is used in the case of powers of attorneys, property transfers, and all the documents relating to contracts where the verification of the signer is important.

The acknowledgement goes as:

On _____, before me, NAME OF NOTARY, appeared NAME OF SIGNER, who proved to me on the basis of satisfactory evidence to be the person whose name is subscribed to the within instrument

Notary Jurat

Notary Jurat is when the signer takes an oath or makes an affirmation. In this case, the notary administers the oath or the affirmation. It is used in the case of affidavits (death affidavits most commonly).

The jurat is usually written as:

Subscribed and sworn to me on this DATE, by NAME OF SIGNER...

What documents need to be notarized?

Certain documents need to be notarized before they can have any legal binding. They include affidavits, authorizing consent of a minor travelling abroad, purchasing and transferring property, making important transactions, and every other document that needs your signature.

A notary makes sure that you are signing the document being well aware of what it may entail. This verifies your identity to prevent fraud. Institutions require notarized documents before they can be used any further. Notarization is a proof that the document is signed by the person himself that acts as a guarantee of its authorization.

Notarized documents are extremely important. Thanks to technology, you can now get documents notarized online which takes less than 5 minutes. Find a reliable source online and connect via a video call and you are good.

You can also visit a public notary to get your document notarized. You can find a notary public, meet them in person with the valid documents, and original ID (some may require proof of identification other than ID) and get your documents notarized.

What does it mean to get a document notarized?

Notarizing documents means that you are declaring that the documents you provided are authentic and facts contained in it are true under the law. Notarization serves as a seal of identification to avoid any confusion in the further process.

When do you need a notary?

You would need a notary whenever required to sign a legal document. Bank documents of certain sort, affidavits, will, affirmation of oaths and pledges etc.

Realtors, business owners, insurance brokers, healthcare and professional service providers need a notary to deter fraud and ensure proper execution of legal matters.

How to get a document notarized?

There are two ways in which you can get your document notarized; meet a notary in person and apply for notarization online.

Meeting a notary in person involves finding a commissioned notary online first. Fill in all the important things of the documents except for signing. You are supposed to sign the document in the presence of a notary that verifies your identity thereby acting as a certified witness. A notary will require a few documents including your valid ID. They will then sign your document and seal it so that it can be used further without any doubts on its authenticity.

Electronic notarizations are exactly the same except that everything is done via digital tools on a video chat. The notary and its client will complete their respective portions with the aid of digital tools. Notary's authorization stamp will be attached to the document once they witness their client signing it. Once notarized, the client may get a print of the document to use it further.

Why should you consider becoming a notary?

Where there is a legal document being signed, there is definitely a notary. Due to the multitude of utilities of notarization, it is safe to say that notaries never run out of work.

1. The market

Considering the sensitivity of legal documents, notaries are always in demand. Be it the affirmation of either an oath or affidavit, notary public is required to approve the signer. The market can never have enough notaries as a legal document is either being signed or prepared every three seconds around the globe.

2. Soloprenuership

If you believe in 'soloprenuership' and absolutely can't work under anyone for that matter, becoming a notary would definitely appeal you. You decide when you work and who to provide your service to. It is a freelance work where you get paid client by client. You can control your work using your phone and can even opt for mobile notarizations, if going out is not an option for you.

3. No hefty investments required at all

You don't need money or any fancy degree to become one. Get yourself enrolled in notary training and trust us that is the only drill you are ever going to face for the rest of your notary career. When it comes to self-owned businesses, it is hard to find one where one can be guaranteed more work than initial investment. Well, now you know one!

4. You can start your own mobile notary business

Electronic notarizations are just like freelance work. You can start your own home-based business. If you are a registered notary, starting a home based notary business would appeal you the most. You can choose when to work and how much every day. You can make good money out of your online work that does not consume much of your time. It could also save you the money that you would otherwise spend on travelling to the client. If you are also trained as a loan signing agent along with the notary public, there are even more benefits attached.

5. Every business needs a notary

The highly competitive realm of business has made it mandatory for every business whether small scale or multinational to have a notary. The intricacies of business deals that have the capacity to either make or break your business need a certified witness. This not only saves businesses from frauds but builds trust that leaves no room for doubts of any sort.

6. Part-time or full-time, you choose!

What is even better is that since you will not be preoccupied with the notary work all day, you get time to invest in other things. You can do any other part-time job that does not drain you that much. Often times, people use certain type of part-time jobs to enhance their skill set for another job. For instance, in certain states where an attorney is permitted to be a notary, part-time notary job can help understand the intricacies of certain legal documents.

7. Fee structure

The amount of fees that you can charge a client varies from state to state. Different states have different upper maximum that you can charge a client. For example in Washington, you can't charge a client more than $10. However, there are states that don't have any upper maximum and it is entirely up to the notary what they charge. Examples of these sates include Alaska, Iowa, Maine, Massachusetts and Tennessee etc.

8. Marketable skill that looks good on your resume

Due to the tremendous demand of notaries in the market, having what it takes to be one will add to a marketable skill in your resume. Every kind of business needs a notary in its workplace these days. Having an employee who is a notary at the same time can be beneficial in two ways; (a) you will be able to notarize documents for your boss and co-workers that will strengthen your position at work (b) People tend to trust their legal documents authentication with a person who is equipped with notary skills.

9. You can opt it as community work

If money is not an incentive for you and giving back to your community is one of your priorities then notary is the right way to go about it. Provision of legal papers' authentication free of cost is a huge thing you can do for someone in a dire need of it. Think of the groups of people who can't go for notarizations because it is beyond their pocket. These groups include college students, elderly, and homeless and physically or mentally impaired etc.

10. Providing a valued service

By administering people's oaths and affirmations and verifying their identities while signing important documents, you are minimizing the chances of scams and forgery. Many important deals concerning transactions and legal documents are contingent upon the authentication of the notaries. It is a valuable service that you are providing your community with. It adds to a remarkable credential to your skillset wherever you apply.

Misconceptions about Notaries

Since notaries provide services that can be easily confused with an attorney's, many people have troubling conceptions of it.

Let's discuss a few common ones just so we are clear:

Notaries decide what they charge

No, they don't. The fee that they are required to charge is usually set by state law. However digital notarizations may ask for additional fees in case of travelling. The travelling expenses are to be decided by the notary himself.

Notaries are bound to notarize documents they are presented with

This is also not true. A notary can refuse to notarize a document. The reasons may include:

- Suspicion of a scam
- Signer's identity can't be verified
- The signer's consent in signing the document is questionable

However, the reasons for which a notary can't refuse include: discrimination on the basis of ethnicity, race, religion, nationality etc.

Notaries can give legal advice

Notaries can't give legal advice as they are forbidden to do so by law unless they are an attorney.

Anyone can become a notary

Becoming a notary is not hard but that, in no way, means that anyone can become one. Apart from the basic prerequisites e.g. 18 years of age (at least), no criminal record, legal resident of the state, and certain other requirements as well which vary from state to state.

Notarization makes a document authentic and legal completely

It is encouraged that a notary must make sure that no fraud or scam is taking place but notarization does not make any document legal. It merely attests the signer's identity and presence for signing the document. A notary should know what the document is for. It is not the duty of a notary to make sure that the document is either legal or true.

How do I become a notary?

More than 4.4 million people in America are becoming notaries. A significant number of people opting to get into this profession is due to its increased utility. If not more, it adds to a marketable skill in your resume that looks good for every kind of job.

You can run your notary agent business part time on your phone and earn through electronic notarizations if travelling and meeting clients in person is a problem for you.

Who can become a notary?

The qualifications for becoming a notary vary from state to state. In USA, it is easy to become a notary in most of the states (38 out of 50). The majority of states won't require you to pass an exam or get any formal training for it.

One of the most important prerequisites is that you must be at least 18 years of age.

5 out of 50 states require you to take a proper notary public course. These courses are available online and are easily accessed.

7 out of 50 require a test, two of which are open book.

Here is your step by step guide to become a notary:

The training

One of the most important things you should decide initially is whether you want to go for a proper legal training or not. Since a notary is not a legal attorney, you do not require a JD or law degree to become one. However, you may want to add a formal training to enhance your skill set. You can also opt for a professional training which is handy and more practical.

Your criminal record

After age, the next most important thing to consider is your criminal record. Under United States law, people with criminal records are not immediately disqualified for the job. In case of minor crimes, you may stand a good chance of still being considered for the job. But when it comes to crimes with substantial amount of harm attached, it could have a huge impact. It could significantly diminish your chances by raising questions on your capabilities. For instance in states such as New York and Texas, you are not eligible to become a notary if previously charged with a felony.

For California, you must not be convicted with a felony that is incompatible with the duties of a notary. For example, you must not have a previous record of committing a fraud, tax evasion or burglary etc.

In Florida, you are eligible if you were a convicted felon but have your civil rights restored.

For Kansas, you are not eligible if previously convicted or have your license revoked.

So, in majority of the states, criminal record is carefully evaluated before considering one for becoming a notary.

English language requirement

Since English is a language frequently spoken and understood in almost all the states, it is a requirement in many states for applying for notary public.

For instance in Kentucky and Kansas, the applicant must be able to understand, read and write in English.

Legal Residence

In order to become a notary public in any state, you must be a resident of the respective state. It is a prerequisite in almost all the states.

Make sure you have a proof of your legal residence before you apply. You may not be eligible otherwise.

Also, if you are not a U.S citizen it is not a problem. The only thing that matters in this regard is your legal residence in the respective state.

Notary public courses and classes

Certain states ask you to take notary public courses before you can apply to become one. For instance in California, you are required to take the course which is also available online for $69. So, you can take the course while sitting at home.

Colorado, Oregon, North Carolina and California are those few sates that ask for specialized training (classes that run from three to six hours costing you around $100-150 approximately) for becoming a licensed notary public.

For Florida, the applicants are required to complete a three hour course offered by the state with a training program (approved by the Executive Office of the Governor).

States such as Kansas and Kentucky don't not require any prior educational course or training in the respective field.

Special Exams

In many states, exams are conducted that must be taken by the applicants. The states where taking the exam is mandatory include Louisiana, Maine, Nebraska, New York, California, North Carolina, Colorado, Connecticut, Oregon, Hawaii, and District of Columbia. States such as Louisiana let you skip it if you have the license to practice law in the state.

The exam, in majority of the states, comprises of 30 multiple choice questions. The applicants get 50 minutes to complete it. You are required to score 70% to pass the exam. You can give the exam twice but not in the same month. If you fail, a free re-take anytime (except in the same month) can be availed.

The results are mailed to the postal and mailing address after 15 days.

The crucial part; Licensing

Just as you get a license to drive after passing a driving test, becoming a legalized notary also entails a valid license. Different states have different authorities to obtain license from.

For instance, in California, Office of Secretary of State, Business Programs Division, Notary Public Section handles the applications. Once you fill in the application, the administration evaluates and grants you the license.

Department of State handles the application process in Florida. Notaries are appointed by the Governor. The Executive Office of the Governor is also in charge of dismissing a notary for their misconduct.

In New Jersey, Secretary of Treasury handles the applications for notaries public.

The application for notary public can be obtained from the state department responsible for licensing.

Filling the application

The application generally inquires about your personal information. In some states you may be asked about your previous experience as a notary public (if any). Carefully fill the application and make sure you don't enter any inaccurate information regarding your address or contact number.

You will be charged a fee for the application which varies from state to state.

The cost

For Florida, the application fee is $39. In California, the total cost of the application and the exam is $40. Additional costs may vary depending on the vendor you choose for the required training course, surety bond, live scan background check, passport photo,

Notary supplies, and county clerk bond and oath of office filing fees.

For the application in the state of Kentucky, $30 will be charged. Other states may cost you around $25 or more.

In the case of acceptance of the application

If your application gets accepted, you are supposed to return the commission certificate to the appropriate office. After sending the commission certificate, take the oath with the county clerk.

The rejection rate

Your application can also get rejected. There are multiple reasons for it which may vary with each state.

For instance in Florida your application can be rejected because of the following reasons:

- The signature and printed name's mismatch
- The date of birth does not match the state records
- The signature on the form is missing
- For the ones applying for renewal, previous commission number doesn't match
- The 'race' field is left
- The bond form is missing
- Inaccurate driver's license information

This largely covers the possible reasons for rejection in other states as well. You may be asked for a resubmission on rejection.

Complying with the state's laws and policies

Once you become a notary, there are certain important things you must take into consideration. You must read about the notary laws defined by your state once you start practicing your services. An elaborated file of notary laws for each state is available as an open source on the internet.

Establishing an Identity For Your Notary Business

Market yourself

People consider marketing themselves as secondary in notary business. This is where they go wrong. In a world filled with competition at every level, marketing should be one of the initial things you should do.

Once you are done with all the procedures, you have to market yourself. Here are a few ways how you can market efficiently:

Come up with a catchy tagline

One of the best ways to make people remember you is by a tagline. Create a very catchy tagline that sticks in people's head. This will give you an edge over your competitors.

Don't forget business cards

Print out plenty of business cards that you can hand over to your clients and potential ones too. It is one of the most effective ways to help people remember you and contact you easily.

Track your marketing strategies' progress

What good of a strategy is it if it is not giving you any positive results? The only way to find out if your marketing strategy is actually working is by tracking its progress. You can simply ask your client how they got to know about you. Once you know, it gets easier to make adjustments in your marketing policy accordingly.

Advertise on social media

Platforms like Facebook, Twitter and LinkedIn can be effectively used to advertise your business. You can post your business oriented articles, FAQs and can even ask for feedbacks there. You can target new clients using Facebook. Check what they post which will help you understand them better. This makes the initial contact easier giving you an edge while engaging with them.

Comply with your state's policy about advertising

Most importantly, make sure you comply with your state laws as to how you can and cannot advertise. Certain states have laws that define how notaries must not advertise. For instance, the use of term 'notario' (a Spanish word) is prohibited in U.S because the term implies a role that entails more legal power compared to U.S notary public's actual power.

Protecting Yourself As a Business
The surety bond and why do you need it?

A surety bond is a kind of contractual guarantee that you pay anyone if you fail to discharge your duties as a notary. It must not be mistaken as a type of insurance because it protects the public, not you. Different states have different bond fees. A Bond fee is taken from a surety company. Any loss to the bond must be paid back to the surety company. The surety company can also ask you for additional cost that it may need to pay in order to defend the bond.

California requires a $15,000 surety bond from a surety company that is authorized to work in the state. For Florida and Kentucky, it is $7,500 and $1,000 respectively.

Errors and omissions insurance

Many people purchase errors and omissions insurance policy in order to protect themselves from the legal expenses. Errors and omissions insurance is not a prerequisite in majority of states. It is up to the notaries if they want to get it or not.

Basically, it serves as insurance in case you make an unintentional mistake or a false claim is made against you. It covers your legal fees and damages up to the coverage you select. Errors and Omissions insurance policy also covers the attorney fees in case you are asked to defend yourself in the court against the lawsuit filed against you.

Notary commission

Term used for the office of a notary public is called a notary commission. Notaries divisions are held in charge for appointing notary public in different states of U.S. Individuals usually serve as a notary public for the state they reside in but they can also be a part of dual commissions; one for their residential state and other for their neighboring state where they need to travel to in order to perform notary acts.

Notary commissions serve for four years in almost all of the states. However, these commissions can be suspended, revoked or terminated before completing their term in case of violations or any sort of misconduct.

Requirements for Notary Commission

Florida, Kentucky and many other states included don't require you to take an exam when applying for notary commission. For California, the applicants are supposed to pass an exam for it.

The applicants are however, supposed to pay a fee around $10 in most of the states for the notary commission application.

Notary Commission expiration and what follows it

Notary commission expires after four years. Once expired, you need to get it renewed as soon as possible.

For renewal candidates are supposed to submit an application. The renewal procedures differ in various states. For example, in California, the applicants are supposed to retake the exam and do a three hour refresher course before they can apply for a renewal. The exam is conducted by Cooperative Personal Services (for California). The list of approved education providers can be obtained by Secretary of State of California.

In Florida, you are not required to take any sort of educational course when applying for the renewal of your commission.

For Kentucky you must submit the application for the renewal four weeks prior to the expiration date of your commission.

The renewal procedures can be technical in each state. Therefore, make sure you are well aware of all the intricacies as soon as your commission expiration date comes closer. To be on a safer side, start reading on the renewal process of your state at least two months prior to your commission expiration date.

NOTARY SUPPLIES

Notary supplies are basically the stationery that you will need for notarizing documents.

1. Notary seal

Official Notary seal is the first and foremost thing to get once you become a notary. You need a rubber stamp that uses photographically reproducible ink. You will use this stamp (your very own notary seal) while notarizing signatures on the documents.

In Florida, the Secretary of State issues you the approval to buy a notary seal from a state-approved vendor. You cannot buy stamp from unauthorized sources such as any stationery store or online on eBay. Make sure that the stamp you buy does not bleed before or after the use as in leaves a very bad impression on your client as well as it looks highly unprofessional. County officials can also reject documents due to smudging. That is a huge deal, right? Save yourself from that grind and invest in a good stamp for once and for all.

Buy a stamp that is durable and has a high quality. Invest once in good stationery and you are good. The type of stamp you use tells a lot about how seriously you take your job. It is also recommended that you mention your commission expiration date on your seal.

2. A journal of notarial acts

A well bound journal is another important thing in your notary supply cart. Although only a few states ask you to record every notarization you make, it is strongly recommended that to keep a record. It acts as a proof of all the notarizations that you have performed so far that protects you from any false allegation of negligence.

Get a journal with numbered pages with tamper proof sewn construction. This will help you to easily identify the missing pages of the journal. This prevents you from any type of fraud. Ordinary glued or stapled notebooks do not offer the same level of security.

3. ID checking guide

If you perform electronic notarizations or are a retail notary, you will need an ID checking guide. It is important because you are constantly dealing with clients from different set up and background, unlike the notaries dealing with the clients from the same regional set up.

How to Stay Organized?

Applying for notary public can be crucial if you don't pay attention to every detail. Trust us, you don't want to be among that group of the people who gather their documents haphazardly and are submitting things at the last minute. Even a single signature you missed out can ask you for the resubmission of the application which is seriously very exhausting.

Follow our recap with the checklist of all the important stuff you will need at every step to nail the application submission process:

1. Make sure meet all the requirements
   - Age limit
   - Residence in the respective state
   - No criminal record (civil rights restored
2. Certifications that you require
   - Pass the exam if your state requires it
   - Get enrolled in the notary public course if your state requires it
3. Complete the application form
   - Fill in all the important information
   - Double check your personal information e.g. postal address, house phone number, business phone number etc.
   - Attach your most recent passport size pictures (get a new one if necessary)
   - Write clearly. Illegible handwriting leaves room for manipulation of the information you provided
   - Use a pen that does not smudge.

4. Do a background check
    - Submit the request for live scan service form with your fingerprints.
5. Get your commission certificate from the state.
    - Go to the appropriate department to receive your commission certificate.
6. Get your surety bond from a reliable agency
    - Within 30 days of your commission date, file your bond and oath with a county clerk where your principal business is located
11. Get your notary supplies
    - Purchase a stamp (high quality and durable)
    - Get a tamper free journal
    - ID checking guide (for electronic and retail notaries)
12. Get an errors and omissions insurance
13. Get additional training (if you are interested) by enrolling yourself in related courses.

THE CHECKLIST TO BECOME A NOTARY

Grab a pen and a paper and make sure you check all the items from our checklist to successfully complete the process of becoming a notary.

- ✓ Course or exam enrollment (if required)
- ✓ Application
- ✓ Commission certificate
- ✓ Surety bond
- ✓ Errors and omissions insurance
- ✓ Notary supplies

Frequently Asked Questions

What to do in case your personal information changes?

In case your residential address, phone number, business phone number changes, you are supposed to notify the Department of State in writing about it. You must also report if your criminal record changes as hiding it can have some serious repercussions.

What to do if your legal name changes?

In case you get married or decide to change your legal name for other reasons you must contact the bonding agency that handled your application as soon as possible. You can request an amended commission from the Department of State. It will cost you around $25. You can use your old name until you receive your amended commission.

What kind of businesses benefit from having a notary on staff?

Having a notary on staff can be extremely beneficial for your company. The type of businesses that benefit the most include insurance companies, real estate companies, construction companies, mortgage companies and all levels of schools.

Can one perform notarial acts in other counties?

Since a notary public has a statewide jurisdiction, they can perform notarizations in other counties as well.

Can you notarize for your spouse or relatives?

You can notarize for your spouse or relative as long as you don't have any financial or beneficial interest in the transaction.

Can notaries change the instrument they notarize?

A notary public can correct acknowledgement certificate but is not authorized to change, alter or draft any instrument.

Can attorneys be notaries?

Attorneys can be notaries and can notarize legal documents of their clients as long as their name is not mentioned in it and they do not have any vested interest (financial or beneficial) in it.

Conclusion

Becoming a notary gives you an edge over others in the job market. A valuable skill that is always in demand in this highly competitive job market can provide you a multitude of opportunities. You can never be out of work if you are a notary.

The process of becoming a notary may seem like a grind at first but trust us it is not. Follow our guideline and we bet you won't regret it later.

STARTING YOUR OWN NOTARY BUSINESS

One of the major positives about starting your own notary business is the least amount of investment that is needed. You can invest as little as getting a notary certificate and buying notary supplies and start your notary career. Although notaries begin with charging as less as 50 cents per signature but as soon as you acquire the level of a loan signing agent, the figure can massively increase.

Initially you have two options; you can either choose to work only through your phone and build your name from the online services or you can develop a business of one on one notarizations building a firm relationship of trust with your clients. Either way, the perks await you!

Before you start…

Before you start your very own self-owned notary business make sure that there is a demand for it. Understanding market before stepping into it is a wise thing to do. Although, notaries always find work but that does not provide you the guarantee of getting work. If you live in a less populated area where there are already a couple of notaries present, you may not want to start your own business.

Choose what type of business you want to develop

One of the prerequisites of starting your own business regardless of any sort is defining its nature. You need to be clearheaded about the type of business you want to develop. You can either start one from the scratch and be the sole runner of your own business or do a sort of partnership with a colleague. A third option could be that you start your own business and ask a colleague to help you out in some paperwork or legal intricacies and offer him a share in your business. In this way, you will have another person to help you out with different things. This will divide the burden (well, since it is your business, you will always be having more work to do) of work up to some extent at the very least. But if you think that you have got what it takes to start and run a business and become a 'solopreneur' then go ahead!

There are different elements that you would want to consider.

Here is a list:

Is it going to be part-time or full-time?

Decide whether you have got what it takes to be a full type notary business operator or not. If you want to pursue notary business as your ultimate career or the only career that you would want to focus for a particular period of time then why not give a shot at full-time? Full-time businesses require utmost commitment from the owner. You will need to give it proper time and focus that it demands in order to succeed with it. No pain, no gain!

However if you want to adopt notary business for an additional income then part-time should be your call. If your primary focus is on, let's say, some other job and you want to use some extra cash for a vacation or an upcoming big thing that you planned for yourself, part-time notary business could really give you a kick start. You attention will be divided and you can set your own timings for the part-time notary business without having to pull some extra strings.

What is your business budget?

Whenever you think of starting a business, the first thing that pops up is the capital. Before moving forward with anything else, you need to assess the budget you are going to work with. Once you are clear about the finances, you will have to devise other things accordingly. The stationery, place, travel cost and other things that need to be financed have to be carefully planned out so that you do not run out of the budget. Always keep the worst case scenarios in mind. You need to have some extra cash in the cases of emergencies so that you do not have to knock at every door for your misery.

Starting your own business is not a piece of cake and handling finances surely is not either.

Is it going to be an online business or a retail one?

Now comes the next big question, will you opt for a mobile notary business or the retail one? The two types have different variables attached as the market and the strategies for excelling in both also vary.

Mobile notary business

Many people will find that part-time notary business goes perfectly well with online business. Since it works just like freelance and freelance work is mostly part-time then why not pair part-time self-owned notary business with online platform? And we say that is an excellent choice.

In order to set up your mobile notary business, the only kind of hefty investment you need is the time. In the beginning, you will have to invest more of your time in order to lay a good foundation of your business. As you start getting more clients, the time that you invest in the business will make you dollars.

Devising a plan

Since, your business is up there online, your site can be either a real dealer maker or breaker. Before you get into any more intricate details, write a business plan.

You may not pay much heed to writing an extensive one but we suggest you give a thought as to how you want your business to be displayed for your clients. In this highly competitive globalized market, it is a matter of a few seconds for the clients to view multitude of options before settling on the one that suits them the most.

The business plan should include:

- Business hours when you work
- Your specialties that set you apart from others in the market
- Your expected expenses
- Your goals

A comprehensive and well thought out business plan serves as a future guide that makes it easy for people running businesses to choose efficiently between different types of works they are presented with. It also serves as a guide while framing the marketing/advertising strategies in order to achieve the set goal or target.

Seeking help of a professional

A lot of times, people who start an online business, do so under the mentorship of an expert. Online platforms make it extremely easy for you to get connected to professionals through social media and ask for their help. There are various discussion groups where you could ask for one. Even freelancing websites might help you out in this regard. You can even pay mentors or professional to give you a useful business advice or even ask them to help you build your business.

However, this can be a tricky task. You will find a multitude of profiles pop up and choosing the right one can be quite a task. Make sure that the one you choose knows about the laws of your state and has adequate experience. Look through their profile and find out reviews of their current work regardless of its type.

Bringing diversity in your work

Along with your notary services, it is always good to have a non-notary skill set. Consider non-notary works that could complement your services. For instance if you have done a crash course about understanding how laws work or have attended law-oriented workshops, your profile automatically will give you an edge over others.

A distinctive skill set that complements your notary work reflects how effectively as well as efficiently can you be when it comes to professional work. It looks good on your resume.

Time schedule

One of the best things about self-owned businesses is the liberty of choosing the time slot that suits you the best. However, some kinds of self-owned businesses require a substantial part of your time. For a notary self-owned business, you don't have to worry about it. When to work and for how long? It is all up to you.

When it comes to mobile notary business, the life gets even easier. Just like freelance work, you get to decide which client to take.

For a well-organized and efficiently managed business, set time in which you will work. This will provide you with a proper working hour routine. A set schedule for work is always a good idea if you are the owner of a business.

CHECKLIST FOR GETTING YOURSELF ORGANIZED

- ✓ Settle on a budget
- ✓ Pick a time slot
- ✓ Make a plan
- ✓ Set your target
- ✓ Keep a record of your work in a journal
- ✓ Review your work every month
- ✓ Tick the above things off your list and stick to your plan

BUILDING YOUR BRAND

A successful business is always consistent with its brand name. Branding is important for small businesses as much as it is for big corporate firms.

For those of you who don't know, let us tell you what branding actually is. Branding is more or less the identity of a business. It defines a business' core values. It is how your audience perceives your business. We all will agree that today's market has become crowded with not just similar businesses but competitive ones. Due to overwhelming number of options available out there, the consumers have become savvy. They can tell whether you are just trying to sell your brand or it is actually something that you would do.

So building your brand is crucial and deserves your utmost focus. A brand that is strategically built will buy its way into the market quite successfully.

Still confused about how to build your brand, worry not! We will tell you how.

Here is how:

What sets you apart from other similar businesses?

One of the most initial things you need to define is what is that one thing that sets you part from others in the market? It is important because the clients won't choose you because you are providing the basic service they need, every other business will have it. The clients are always looking for the best deal they can get.

Take a moment or as much time as you want to decide for once about what will you be providing and how will you do it? If you are running a notary business that will require you to meet clients in person to perform notarization then decide how much of the travelling cost will your client be paying? Are you going to give any discount to the clients that have come to you on their friend's recommendation (previously, your client)? This will give you an edge over others in the market. An appealing offer attracts a good deal of clients.

What drives your business?

Is it love for serving people or the target that you have set for yourself? For marketing purposes, you will have a website developed for your business. A good mission statement that reflects your core values is essential for every kind or business regardless of its financial limitations.

Make your clients your permanent clients

Always try that your clients come back to you. When you get a client, try your best to always be up to the mark so that the client does not get disappointed. Be punctual. Try to be humble yet professional. Once you are successful in developing a good relationship with your client, the chances are that your client will return to you whenever they need the service again. So make sure you leave a good impression on every client you work with.

Here are a couple of tips to make help you out:

- Speak in a consistent tone as it sounds more professional
- Always dress professionally.

Do not copy other similar businesses in the market

One of the reasons behind your business fallout could be because you appear very similar to the other brand. Do not try to mimic other businesses that you idealize. It is completely fine to draw inspirations from other businesses but imitating their brand would not do any good for your business. Don't lose your customers and establish a distinct identity.

Your brand should reflect your values

You may think that a notary business should not be taken as seriously as other businesses that have a greater impact but this is not true. A successful notary business where you will always have clients coming to you is the one where you respect your clients as much as you would want your brand or work to be respected. Your work's value is contingent upon your behavior with your clients. If your core values are in line with your client's (as in you respect your client and in turn get valued proportionately), your brand will surely earn a good name.

Establish a name

With the above things kept in mind, establish a name for your brand. Establishing a name that is unique yet sends a clear message about what you offer is extremely important. You should choose a name that is unique and reflects your core values. Even if you want to keep your notary business low key (which we think you should not as it can be a good source of earning), you have to focus on a distinctive name that will help your customers in finding you.

Establishing a name does not only mean to choose a name for your brand but building it strategically to attract more customers. If you focus on dealing with every customer professionally and ethically, it will automatically establish a good repute of your work. From a good reputation, stems a successful business.

Create a logo

Logo is that distinctive mark with which your brand gets recognition. It is very important for the branding of your business. Creating a logo that depicts the true essence of your brand is essential. It is something that your customers will remember after they have left. Be very careful when designing your logo (or getting it designed). First thing you are going to be judged on is your logo. It gives your potential customers an idea about your identity.

Here is what you should consider while creating your business logo:

Your logo needs to be eye-catching and unique at the same time

A good logo attracts new customers. It is not necessary that the logo you wish to choose for your notary business needs to incorporate something 'notary related'. Consider other eye-catching logos. A fast food chain can have a food logo but do all the fast food chains have food incorporated in their logos? So, while choosing what to go for in your logo, do not feel restricted by limited 'strictly business' options.

Your logo does not need to have a picture

We know that graphics are aesthetically pleasing but they are not a must in a logo. If you can't think of a picture that depicts your brand, try thinking of a word or a style in which your brand name can be written to form a logo. Do not try too hard to make your logo look attractive. Try to keep it simple.

Know the color psychology

Different types of businesses incorporate different colors in their logos due to the significance each color withholds. For instance, you will notice that many food chains have red color in their logo. Red color signifies hunger. When it comes to law and justice, black and white is majorly chosen as it looks more serious.

You will find multitude of things associated with different colors. Give a thorough study to the color significance before finalizing.

Remember once you create a logo, there is no turning back. Give it your best shot!

Staying consistent with your brand matters!

You will probably be thinking that why do we keep on saying that over and over again. Simple. Because it is that important. Brand consistency is a pattern that you follow with which your clients are able to see how ingenious you are to your name. A brand that provides what it offers without ever disappointing is a brand that is consistent.

Here is how you can maintain brand consistency:

Write down your brand strategy

One of the key things to bring brand consistency is by preparing a guideline for marketing at different platforms. This guideline will be something that you would always follow. This will bring consistency in the way you advertise. You will be able to send out a clear message that is not open to different interpretations of the people.

Make sure that the guidelines that you decide to go on with, are coherent with company's mission and vision. It is important as it also forms an integral part of brand consistency.

Develop your marketing strategy

There are plenty of online platforms that can be used for online marketing. Once you understand your target clients, you would know which platforms to publicize on. Choose those platforms that have a greater outreach so that your message is spread across the maximum number of people. Create social media cover photos with your logo on them for your clients. The photos do not need to be work-oriented. You can create interesting photos as in FAQs and put your logo on each of the photos. Be careful about using your logo. Do not use it too much as it is generally not taken that well.

Here is what you should do:

- Evaluate your target audience
- Choose social media platforms on which you want to publicize
- Create appropriate content
- Spread the word without overdoing it

Give souvenirs to your clients if possible

Souvenir can be anything; a pen, a notebook, a sticker or a calendar etc. If your budget allows you, think of something of a utility that you can give to your clients with your brand's logo on it. It will serve as a reminder of the services you provided and promote your business among their social circle. A souvenir generally gets everyone excited whether it is just a pen or a calendar.

You can think about it even after some time in the business when you think you have adequate finance. Stationery souvenirs are generally less costly when bought in a bulk. You can even buy plain notepads in bulk from a retailer and use your stamp to impression your logo on it. This will save you the printing cost. Of course, we think that getting them printed by yourself is a better idea but if you are running on a low budget then why not?

Finding clients

One of the trickiest things in the business is looking for clients. Since you know what you are doing quite well (well, we assume you do because you are thinking of starting your own business), knowing your target clients won't be that hard. In a notary business, you will have clients from diverse ranges. People will come to you for their will, affidavits, bank statements, business deals, real estate property, marriage and what not.

You are people's deal verifier. And that is a big thing.

The legal documents sealing

Many of your clients will want you to verify their legal documents from you. For instance, children who are below 18 years of age and want to get a passport would need you. People who want to go ahead with an important deal would want to come to you to verify their legal documents.

Wills are signed under the presence of a notary who later seals it with their notarization.

Property business

Even transferring property within a family needs to be notarized to prevent any future conflicts. Realtors, every now and then need notaries to run their business smoothly without any violation of property and consent laws.

Many real estate businesses have at least one person on board with them that knows notarization and has a legal license for it. This makes it even easier for them to run their business and make deals efficiently.

Weddings

Yes, notaries can also become wedding officiants. Many states like Nevada, Florida and South Carolina allow the notaries to perform the duties of a wedding officiant. You can become an ordained minister online. Internet ordination is completely legal and even the people who are not notaries can become registered or ordained minister.

Notaries can add wedding officiant in the services they provide. This brings diversity in the work they deal with. Wedding ceremonies need officiants all the time. You can earn good money once you start officiating weddings as well.

Officiating a wedding opens up more channels; if the family from the wedding liked your services, they would may want you to notarize their other documents. This builds their trust and who knows you may end up notarizing their documents for life.

You can also leave your business card or brochure or any souvenir (a pen, desk calendar etc.) at a few important tables. This way, you can market yourself at work.

You can even ask the couple if they require any legal name change. You can notarize the legal name change for them. That is a good deal of work from a single client, right?

So go ahead and add wedding officiant services to your services.

Virtual bankruptcy assistant services

A virtual bankruptcy assistant is an independent contractor that works with different consumer bankruptcy attorneys to prepare petitions. Notaries can be virtual bankruptcy assistants you can either choose to work with agencies that are always in need of tech savvies or start doing it on your own. You can provide virtual bankruptcy services to your clients. You will need to be well-informed and equipped with latest technologies to do the work efficiently.

Keep in mind that your clients know their business way too well and since you are going to be their virtual assistant, you have a good deal of responsibility to deal with.

Things to consider after you have developed your own notary business

Now that you have invested your capital and labor in creating a business, there are certain things that you have got to do in order to sustain your business.

Here is what is important:

Creating alliances

For small businesses, strategic alliances hold immense importance. It provides you the opportunity to share resources. You can do a partnership with a friend or a colleague or even a company. This will divide the burden of finances as well as work. Shortage of cash could be problem for the beginners who are the sole runners of a business.

Benefits

Small business owners are, many a time, limited by the resources they have. If you have started a business on your own and now do not even have a penny to spend on its marketing, how do you think your business will do in this highly competitive market? Lack of marketing could be a huge hindrance. If you have invested a lot of your capital in building a business, its failure could be a huge set back. In cases where small business owners have limited resources, creating strategic alliances are always a good idea.

You can either go for a 50/50 partnership or offer a part of the share to the one you want to have an alliance with. This is also beneficial in terms of intellectual power. You have another expert working with you and increasing the pool of ideas. A different perspective is always good as it can prepare you for the future challenges that you may have to face.

You can also gain different types of skill sets with alliances. Your ally's skill sets may compliment yours and together to can make a good team. You can help polish each other's strengths.

You can expand the pool of your services with alliances. Certain services that you can't provide may be your ally's strong area. The services that you and your ally can provide can amount a wide range expanding your pool of overall services.

In order to create alliances that are beneficial to both the companies, start networking. You can look for your potential partner on social media and if you like any, you can have a one on one conversation.

Do not hesitate asking for the money you earned

Yes, working with big corporations can be intimidating at times. You may hesitate while asking for money. But we say, don't. Not even out of courtesy. This is especially for virtual bankruptcy assistants. Read the company's payment policy first. Send them a notice when the payment is late. Make sure you keep a paper trial.

Keep a record of everything; the day you contacted the company for payment, the person who took your message and other details. It will facilitate you in case any false claim is made.

You should send the company a final notice letter in case of delay of the payment. You can even ask your attorney to send the notice on your behalf. In that letter, clearly state the due date of the payment, the contract made and what will be your point of action if the payment is not made. Also, send the letter through a certified mail so that you have the proof of it (you have got to be safe from all the sides)

Final Thoughts

Becoming a notary has its perks. Not only does it enhance your skill set but it will always find you work in almost any kind of business. Even if you can't join a company as a notary, there are chances that your company might need one for notarizing important statements, contracts and other legal documents.

However, the state in which you want to become a notary matters a lot. You have to make sure that you meet your state's requirements to become a notary.

Follow our guidelines and it won't be a grind for you.

Looking To Learn More

Starting a successful Notary Business takes more information and skills than can be put in one book. To help give you all the resources that you need we have partnered with the top provider for online Notary material, Notary.net.

Visit https://notary.net/?ref=175 **to receive special access to all the insider secrets**

ABOUT THE AUTHOR

Jackson Carter is a self-published author who enjoys developing hobbies from a variety of different areas. His main way of learning is through writing books for other.

CAN I ASK A FAVOR?

If you enjoyed this book, found it useful or otherwise then I'd really appreciate it if you would post a short review on Amazon. I do read all the reviews personally so that I can continually write what people are wanting.

Thanks for your support!

Made in the USA
Middletown, DE
29 November 2023